C000177675

To a very special daddy:

From:

For Michael.
You are our hero every day.

My Daddy Is My Hero

First edition February 2022
Illustration and design by Asya Kaznacheeva

ISBN 978-1-8382893-3-1

My Daddy Is My Hero

Written by
Emma Ledden

Illustrated by
Asya Kaznacheeva

My daddy is the greatest,
so brave and strong and true.

When I grow up,

I want to be just like him,
through and through.

My dad knows all about football,
he even has a favourite team.

When they're on the TV,
well, he sometimes shouts and screams!

When we play together,
he shows me how to pass.
He cheers me on and helps me kick.
He really is first class.

My dad is Mr. Fix It,
no job too big or small.

He has lots of different tools
and a ladder that's really tall!

He changes light bulbs,
fixes shelves, and
other things we need.

He is the best dad in the world.
Mum says, "That's agreed!"

My daddy has a barbeque.
It's in our garden shed.

On sunny days he cooks on it,
a chef's hat on his head.

He stands in our garden for hours,
cooking loads of yummy food.

My daddy is amazing.
He's really a cool dude.

My daddy shows me
how to share and play with others too.
He teaches me about taking turns.
First, it's me, then you!

He tells me about manners,
how to say thank you and please.

Please, please, please!
Please, please!

I tell him he's the greatest dad
and give him a big squeeze.

At Christmas time, I got a bike.
It's shiny, and it's blue.

My dad helps me to ride it,
but I'm wobbly 'cause it's new.

He's really very patient,
and he holds me while I ride.

I know he's very proud of me because his eyes are full of pride.

My dad is very funny.
We laugh and laugh all day,

with funny jokes or silly songs,
he always finds a way.

He's really good at playing games
and Lego building too.

The truth is, when it comes to my dad, there's nothing he can't do.

Every day my daddy
teaches me important stuff -
to ride my bike,

to kick a ball,

to know that I'm enough.

My daddy is my hero.
I admire him most of all,
and when he's by my side,
I feel a hundred feet tall!

ABOUT EMMA

Emma Ledden is a proud Mammy of two boys. She is also a best-selling author, leading international communication coach and television presenter. She loves writing and spending time with her family.
Find her on Instagram @emled1

To small children, their moms are their world. They are the fixers, the co-pilots, the movers and shakers every day. They can find lost stuff, cook, comfort, cure, play and even send their kids to sleep - sometimes!
This book is a celebration of all mammies out there and their superpowers.

Lightning Source UK Ltd.
Milton Keynes UK
UKHW052211150322
400070UK00002B/206